Timeline of the Aztec Empire

1299

The ruler of the city of Culhuacan allows the Aztecs to settle at Tizapan after they are driven out of their previous home by the Tepanecs.

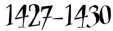

1111

According to legend, the Aztecs travel from their northern homeland of Aztlan.

1427–1430

The Aztecs and other city-states make war against the Tepanec empire, to which they formerly paid tribute.

1250

After roaming the area that is now Mexico, the Aztecs settle near Lake Texcoco.

1431

The Aztec empire is founded by a Triple Alliance among the Aztecs of Tenochtitlan and the cities of Texcoco and Tlacopan.

1325

The Aztecs found the city of Tenochtitlan on an island in Lake Texcoco, having been guided there by a vision.

1492

Christopher Columbus lands at Santo Domingo and becomes the first European to reach the West Indies.

1521

Cuauhtemoc surrenders to Cortés. The Spanish rebuild Tenochtitlan as Mexico City, capital of New Spain.

1519

Spanish nobleman Hernando Cortés lands on the Yucatan peninsula and leads an army to Tenochtitlan. The Spanish bring with them diseases not previously known in Central America, such as smallpox.

1502–1520

Reign of Montezuma II (born ca. 1466), ninth king of Tenochtitlan.

1525

Cuauhtemoc is hanged by the Spanish on the pretext that he was plotting to kill Cortés.

1520

Cortés, allied with enemies of the Aztecs, begins his assault on the empire. Montezuma is killed (it is not clear how). Cuitlahuac, tenth king of Tenochtitlan, dies of smallpox and is succeeded by Cuauhtemoc.

Map of Tenochtitlan

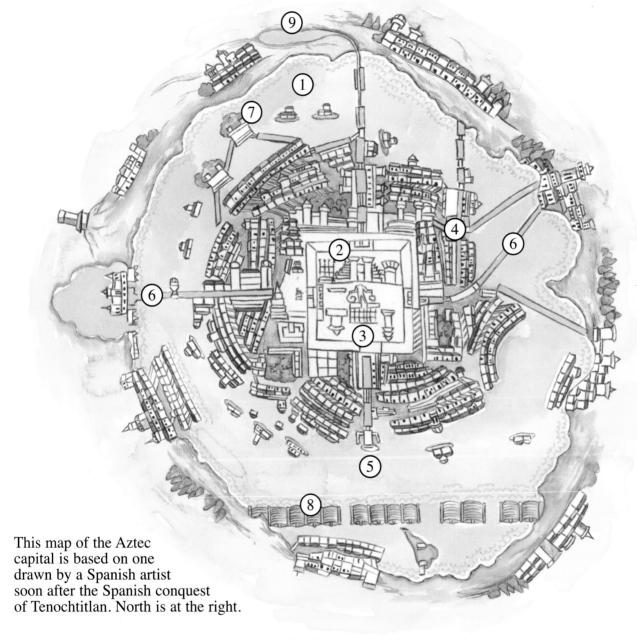

This map of the Aztec
capital is based on one
drawn by a Spanish artist
soon after the Spanish conquest
of Tenochtitlan. North is at the right.

1. Lake Texcoco
2. Temple where sacrifices are made
3. Heads of the sacrificial victims
4. Plaza
5. Temple for prayers

6. Causeways linking islands and shore
7. Montezuma's garden
8. Barrier to protect houses from flooding
9. Spring supplying fresh water to the city

Author:
Fiona Macdonald studied history at
Cambridge University and at the University of
East Anglia, England. She has taught adult
education, and in schools and colleges, and is the
author of numerous books for children on
historical topics.

Artist:
David Antram was born in Brighton, England,
in 1958. He studied at Eastbourne College of Art
and then worked in advertising for 15 years before
becoming a full-time artist. He has illustrated
many children's nonfiction books.

Series Creator:
David Salariya was born in Dundee,
Scotland. He has illustrated a wide range of books
and has created and designed many new series for
publishers both in the UK and overseas. In 1989
he established The Salariya Book Company. He
lives in Brighton with his wife, illustrator Shirley
Willis, and their son, Jonathan.

Editor:
Karen Barker Smith

Assistant Editor:
Stephanie Cole

© The Salariya Book Company Ltd MMXIV
No part of this publication may be reproduced in whole or in
part, or stored in a retrieval system, or transmitted in any form
or by any means, electronic, mechanical, photocopying,
recording, or otherwise, without written permission of the
publisher. For information regarding permission, write to the
copyright holder.

Published in Great Britain in 2014 by
The Salariya Book Company Ltd
25 Marlborough Place, Brighton BN1 1UB

ISBN-13: 978-0-531-27104-9 (lib. bdg.)   978-0-531-23855-4 (pbk.)

All rights reserved.
Published in 2014 in the United States
by Franklin Watts
An imprint of Scholastic Inc.
Published simultaneously in Canada.

A CIP catalog record for this book is available
from the Library of Congress.

Printed and bound in China.
Printed on paper from sustainable sources.
1 2 3 4 5 6 7 8 9 10 R 23 22 21 20 19 18 17 16 15 14

SCHOLASTIC, FRANKLIN WATTS, and associated logos are
trademarks and/or registered trademarks of
Scholastic Inc.

PAPER FROM
SUSTAINABLE
FORESTS

You Wouldn't Want to Be an Aztec Sacrifice!

Written by
Fiona Macdonald

Do you have the heart for it?

Illustrated by
David Antram

Created and designed by
David Salariya

Gruesome Things You'd Rather Not Know

Franklin Watts®
An Imprint of Scholastic Inc.
NEW YORK • TORONTO • LONDON • AUCKLAND • SYDNEY
MEXICO CITY • NEW DELHI • HONG KONG
DANBURY, CONNECTICUT

Contents

Introduction

I t is the late fifteenth century in Mesoamerica, the area where North and South America meet. You live in a prosperous Mexican city that was conquered by the Aztecs in 1428.

The Aztecs are an energetic and warlike people who are now at the height of their power. They arrived in Mexico around 1200. At first they lived peacefully among your people, working as soldiers and servants. They soon made their presence felt more strongly when they fought and won a war against their masters. In 1325, the Aztecs settled on an island in the middle of a swampy lake and built a vast new city called Tenochtitlan.

Since then, the Aztecs have set out to take over all the neighboring lands. They often demand goods from the cities they have conquered. You have also heard that they take captives and kill them as offerings to their gods. The Aztecs can be ruthless when they are seeking captives. One thing you know for sure is that you wouldn't want to be an Aztec sacrifice!

Great Expectations

You are a young man from a noble family in the Central Valley of Mexico. You have a comfortable home, plenty of food, and a happy family. You enjoy strength and good health.

If it weren't for your overlords, the Aztecs, you would be content with your life. The Aztecs are fearsome warriors, and everybody is scared of them. Your servants have heard a rumor that Aztec ambassadors will soon be arriving in your city. They visit conquered peoples every year, and you dread their arrival.

Mesoamerica

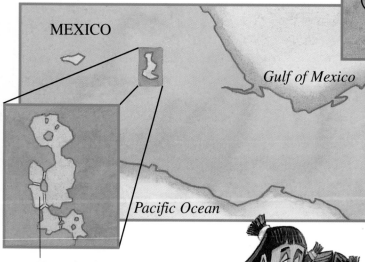

MEXICO

Gulf of Mexico

Pacific Ocean

Tenochtitlan

The Aztecs live in Mesoamerica, where North and South America meet. Their capital city, Tenochtitlan, is built on an island in a lake in the Central Valley of Mexico.

What You Like About Your Life:

YOU GOT MARRIED at age twenty to a girl chosen by your parents. Now you have an adorable baby son.

YOU WERE WELL FED and cared for in childhood, and you grew up healthy. You exercise to keep in shape.

YOU LIVE with your wife and child in your parents' house. It is very large and has a spacious courtyard.

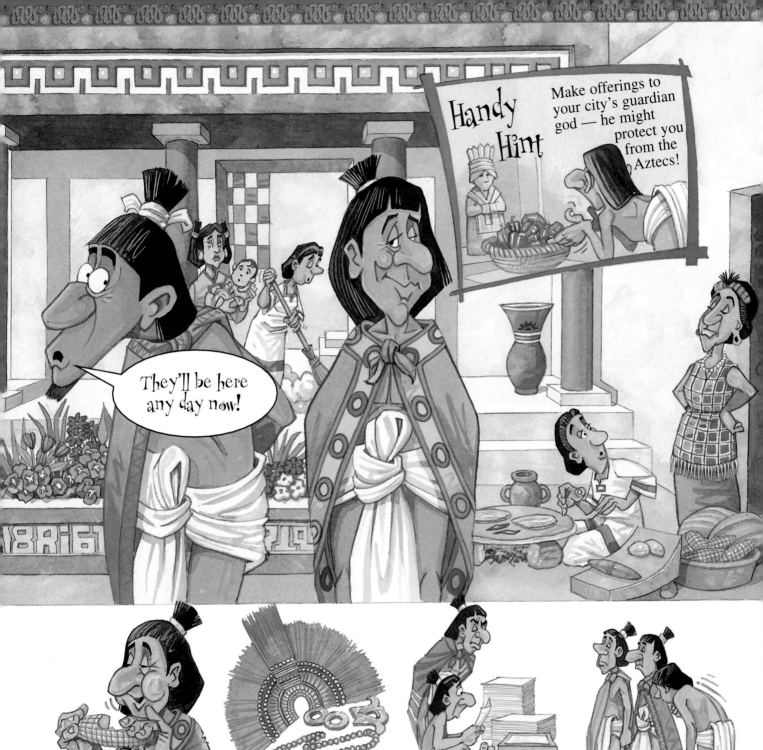

Handy Hint

Make offerings to your city's guardian god — he might protect you from the Aztecs!

They'll be here any day now!

YOU EAT plenty of healthy food, mostly maize and fresh vegetables. You also eat lots of spicy foods.

YOU OWN fine clothes, including a feathered headdress and gold jewelry.

YOU WERE SENT TO SCHOOL as a boy and are able to read, write, and do simple calculations.

YOU ARE RESPECTED by the other citizens because of your nobility.

Hand It Over! Tribute Payments

Picture-Writing

Aztec scribes use picture-writing to draw up lists of all the goods taken as tribute. The most valuable tribute goods include cloaks, blankets, feathers, and cotton.

Finger (a) = 1

Knife (b) = 20

Feather (c) = 400

Shield (d) = 800

It's true! Aztec ambassadors, accompanied by well-armed bodyguards, have just arrived in your city. They come every year to demand goods, known as tribute, which they take back to their capital city. Handing over so much tribute is a great burden for your city — but worse is to come. The Aztecs challenge you to a "flowery war." They want to fight you so they can take some of you captive in battle.

a   b

d

c

400 fine cloaks

20 warrior outfits

440 boxes of cotton

40 shields

22 boxes of beans

400 baskets of chili peppers

What more do you want? Blood?

FLOWERY WARS are not battles where soldiers throw plants at one another. They are ritual wars fought by the Aztecs to win captives for sacrifice.

Thwack!

Handy Hint

Don't try to cheat as you hand over tribute payments. Aztec spies have sharp eyes and keep a careful record of everything.

Get Ready – The Aztecs Are Coming!

Choose Your Weapon:

Bow and arrows

Spear

Battleaxe

Club with obsidian blades

It's time to defend your city — the Aztecs are on the warpath! For days they have been preparing for the flowery war. The great square in the center of their capital city, Tenochtitlan, has resounded to the beat of a huge war drum. Priests have been chanting and dancing on the temple steps, and hundreds of well-trained soldiers have been getting their weapons and armor ready. Led by its famous noble warriors, the Aztec army has marched out of the city and is now making its way toward you! All you can do is prepare your own weapons and wait for the Aztecs to arrive.

You Will Need:

A BOW AND ARROWS, plus a spear, to attack distant enemies, and a sharp battleaxe or warclub for hand-to-hand fighting.

Magic shield

A MAGIC SHIELD decorated with magic patterns. Many soldiers believe the magic will protect them on the battlefield.

PADDED ARMOR. Soak your thickly padded suit in salt water. This will make it even stronger.

10

Disaster! Captured in Battle

Jaguar Knight

Eagle Knight

It's all over! You fought bravely, but you had particularly bad luck — during the battle, you came face to face with a fearsome Eagle Knight. He seemed anxious not to harm you. Instead, he dragged you from the battlefield to join a large group of captives. Now that the battle is over, the terrible truth is beginning to sink in. You might never see your home and family again.

Gotcha!

TOP AZTEC WARRIORS belong to one of two elite brotherhoods — the Jaguar or the Eagle Knights. They wear costumes made from jaguar skin or eagle feathers, which they believe give them the strength of wild beasts.

NOVICE SOLDIERS always have long hair. Be on your guard if you meet one — he'll be eager to get you! Young Aztec warriors are not allowed to cut their hair and arrange it in a top-knot style until they have proved their manhood by killing an enemy or taking captives.

IF YOU ARE INJURED, try traditional remedies. Bathing wounds in salt water kills germs. Raw chili peppers, crushed and rubbed on the skin, help numb pain. Herbal mixtures also act as anesthetics. You can sew wounds up using cactus spines as needles.

Chili peppers

Salt bath

Herbal mixture

Cactus needle

Handy Hint

If you want to make friends with an Aztec warrior, give him flowers. Off-duty warriors like to stroll through the streets, dressed in their best and carrying flowers and herbs.

Take this!

Crack!!!

A Long Desert Walk

IN THE DESERT, even the plants are unfriendly! You'll find no place to hide behind prickly cacti, spindly sage bushes, or tall, thin stalks of maize.

Cacti

Sage

Maize

ith your hands tied behind your back, you have been roped together with many other captives, mostly strong young warriors like yourself. You are hungry, thirsty, and exhausted. The desert dust chokes you, and the hot sun half blinds you as you stumble along a narrow mountain track. You are all being taken to Tenochtitlan, which you can see in the distance. You have heard that it is a magnificent city, full of fine buildings and surrounded by fertile gardens. But any admiring thoughts are far from your mind. You just want to escape!

Even If You Escape...

YOU might die of thirst...

or be driven mad by the loneliness...

or be eaten by wild animals...

or freeze to death overnight...

or even meet an angry Aztec god!

Handpicked! Who Will Be Chosen?

Are You Top Quality?

IF YOU ARE unhealthy, scarred, diseased, ugly, or fat, the Aztecs will not choose you for sacrifice. Instead you will be forced to work as a slave.

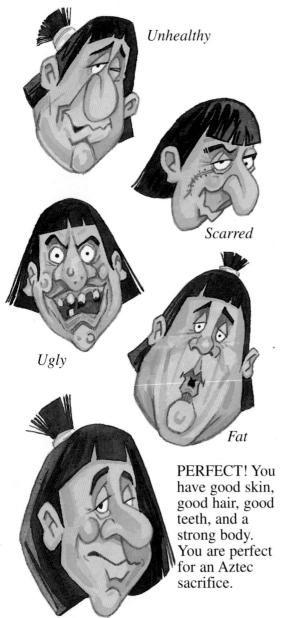

Unhealthy

Scarred

Ugly

Fat

PERFECT! You have good skin, good hair, good teeth, and a strong body. You are perfect for an Aztec sacrifice.

When you reach the Aztec capital city, you are taken to a prison and crammed inside a wooden cage along with other captives. Guards bring you food and water every day. One morning, you are visited by some of the priests from the Aztecs' most important temple. They spend a long time looking at you through the bars of your cage, and the scribes who accompany them write notes on pieces of fig-bark paper. It's a good thing you can't read Aztec picture-writing — otherwise you would learn that your name is being added to the list of prisoners chosen for sacrifice!

AZTEC PRIESTS are sent to temple schools when young and taught to read, write, and calculate (a). They also learn astronomy and religion (b). They endure long nights alone on mountainsides (c) to make them physically and mentally tough. They also help with temple rituals (d).

a

b

c

d

17

A Gift Fit for the Gods

THE AZTECS BELIEVE that the gods will be angry and might destroy the world if they don't offer them sacrifices. Aztec scribes say that this has already happened four times. Previous worlds were destroyed by a hungry tiger, wind, rain, and a flood. Each time the world was reborn. Next time, however, the world will end once and for all in a massive earthquake.

h, no! The guards tell you that the priests have chosen you to be sacrificed as a gift to their gods. You are horrified by this news, but you also understand. Many cultures in Mesoamerica offer human sacrifices to the gods. The gods provide rain, sunshine, and everything else to keep humanity alive, so you must offer them gifts in return. Now, as you sit in your prison cage, only one thought fills your mind. To which god will you be sacrificed?

18

Tezcatlipoca

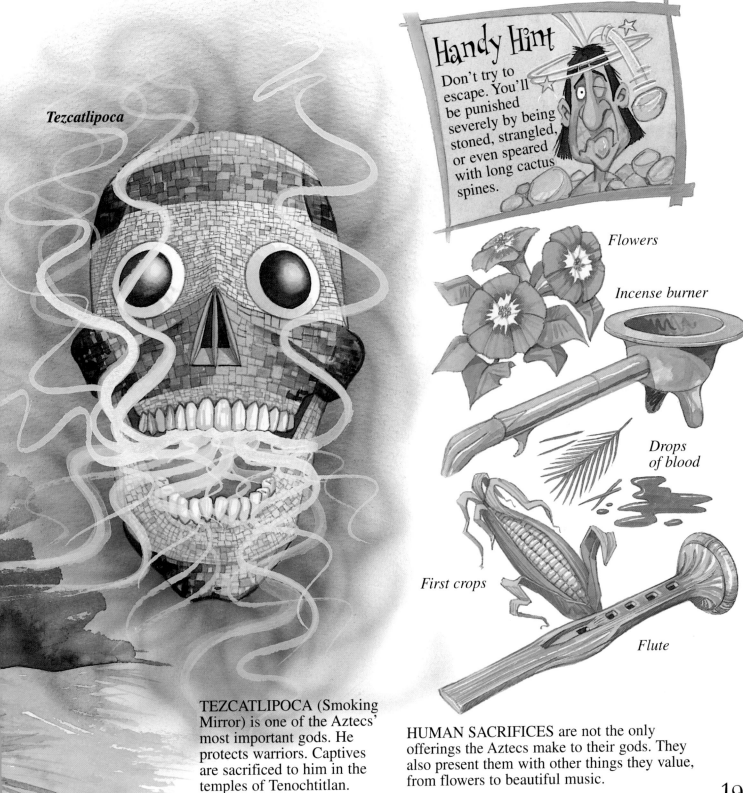

Handy Hint

Don't try to escape. You'll be punished severely by being stoned, strangled, or even speared with long cactus spines.

Flowers

Incense burner

Drops of blood

First crops

Flute

TEZCATLIPOCA (Smoking Mirror) is one of the Aztecs' most important gods. He protects warriors. Captives are sacrificed to him in the temples of Tenochtitlan.

HUMAN SACRIFICES are not the only offerings the Aztecs make to their gods. They also present them with other things they value, from flowers to beautiful music.

19

A Special Day

Soon you learn that the Aztecs are planning a great festival called the New Fire Ceremony. One of their most important festivals, it only happens once every fifty-two years. All lights and fires are put out for five days, and everyone fears the world will end.

AZTEC PRIESTS AND SCRIBES make careful observations of the sun, moon, stars, and planets. They measure time using a calendar that has 260 days. Each year is divided into 13 months, each with 20 days.

Aztec farmers use a different calendar, based on the movements of the sun. It has 360 days, plus 5 extra, unlucky ones. After 73 priests' years and 52 farmers' years, the two calendar cycles end on the same day. This is when the New Fire Ceremony is held.

Priests' calendar

Farmers' calendar

At the end of the five days, priests look for Venus, the evening star, in the sky. When it appears, they sacrifice a captive and light the New Fire on him. Then the Aztecs rejoice.

Don't let it go out!

Handy Hint

Hope to be chosen to play in the ball game. If you win, you'll have a chance of surviving, because only the losing team is sacrificed!

TO CALCULATE days for festivals and sacrifices, Aztec priests and scribes use yet another calendar based on the planet Venus (the evening star). Each Venus year is 584 days long.

THE BALL GAME is a religious ritual as well as a sport. Players keep a rubber ball moving in the court to give energy to the sun.

How Will You Meet Your End?

Most captives are sacrificed by having their hearts cut out with a sharp knife. This is performed so quickly that it is almost painless. Some captives are beheaded, which is also a quick and merciful way to be sacrificed. However, there are also much slower and nastier ways of being killed. You could be thrown into a lake and left to drown, or you could be skinned alive. If you are a warrior, you could be tied to a stone and forced to fight a senior Aztec warrior using weapons made from feathers and wood.

You Might Be:

FLAYED (skinned). In the springtime, captives are sacrificed to Xipe Totec, the god of new young plants. The captives' skins are cut off and used to dress the god's statue.

BEHEADED. Just before harvest, a person the same height as the standing maize is killed by having his head chopped off.

DROWNED. Young people are thrown into lakes as offerings to Tlaloc, the god of water and life-giving rain.

Ha! You'll have to try harder than that!

22

SACRIFICIAL KNIVES are made from flint, obsidian, or semiprecious stone. They are often beautifully decorated with images of the gods. The Aztecs do not know how to make knives from iron or steel, but they are expert stone-workers. These knives are very sharp!

Flint knife

Obsidian knife

Whoosh!

Handy Hint

If you are forced to fight, fight well to bring honor to your family and your city, and to please the gods.

Up the Temple Steps....

Sounds of drumming and chanting echo around the city as the festival approaches. At dawn, the guards make you drink a strange-tasting potion, which makes you feel drowsy. Along with thousands of other captives, you walk to the temple at the center of Tenochtitlan. You see priests with their bodies painted black and red and with wild, matted hair. Behind them, you glimpse fearsome statues of the gods. Walking slowly up the temple steps, you are grabbed by five priests and flung on your back across a sacrificial stone. You see no more...

YOU MIGHT FEEL LOST in the crowds of people. On some occasions, the Aztecs kill huge numbers of captives. It is said that 20,000 men were sacrificed when the Great Temple in the center of Tenochtitlan was dedicated in 1487.

You Are Probably Not Too Scared Because...

AN HERBAL POTION makes you feel drowsy and peaceful.

DRUMMING and chanting lull you into a trance-like state.

AFTER WEEKS in prison, you have forgotten what life was like before.

THE PRIESTS are so awe-inspiring that you feel you have to obey them.

24

Bad hair day

NEXT!

Handy Hint

Thud!

Don't slip on the temple steps! They are terribly steep and will be wet with blood. If you fall, you'll be badly injured and could die a slow, painful death.

?

YOU KNOW that your death will help others — it is a positive act.

What Happens to Your Body?

Honored Offerings:

YOUR HEART, the most precious part of the sacrifice, will be held in a *chac-mool* carved from stone.

YOUR HEAD will be kept in a skull rack outside the temple.

YOUR BLOOD will be poured down the temple steps.

YOUR ARMS AND LEGS will be eaten as a religious feast.

Y ou die quickly and with little pain, but the sacrifice is not over yet. The priests cut your heart from your body and raise it high toward the sky to show it to the gods. Then they place it in a special container, called a *chac-mool*, as an offering to the gods. Next, they cut off your head and display it in a skull rack along with hundreds of others. This gives the temple extra "spirit-power." Finally, your blood is poured down the temple steps, and your limbs are tossed to the crowds of worshipers below. The warrior who captured you collects the limbs and takes them home. He cooks and eats your sacrificed flesh. This is a way of sharing a holy meal and linking heaven and Earth.

THE AZTECS genuinely believe that the sun will only continue to shine if sacrifices are offered to it. They do not view the ritual of sacrifice as cruel or bloodthirsty, because it ensures that life will continue.

Will Your Spirit Become a Butterfly?

Like many other Mesoamerican people, you have always believed that your spirit would live on after death, whatever happened to your body. Because you fought bravely while you were alive and died bravely, too, your spirit will become a beautiful butterfly. It will spend some time on earth, bringing joy to the people who see it. Then, finally, it will fly up to heaven to make its home with the sun. Other people are not so lucky. The Aztecs believe that some unhappy spirits have to make a long, miserable journey through the underworld before they finally perish in hell. Some ghosts are condemned to haunt the Earth forever, bringing fear to all who see them.

SOME SPIRITS, like the ghosts of executed criminals, are said to haunt the streets at night.

Heavens above – thank the gods that's over!

Handy Hint

Feel proud, strong, and free! Every time the Aztecs see a butterfly on Earth, they think of people like you.

THE SPIRITS of women who have died in childbirth are said to terrify travelers at crossroads.

Glossary

Ambassadors
Important officials who are sent abroad to represent their country.

Anesthetic
A drug that makes people sleepy and unable to feel pain.

Astronomy
The study of the sun, moon, stars, and planets.

Aztecs
A Mesoamerican people who lived in central and northern Mexico. They were most powerful between around 1350 and 1520.

Chac-mool
A stone statue in the shape of a dying warrior or water god carrying a dish in his arms. The dish was used to hold blood or hearts from human sacrifices.

Dedicated
Given to, or named for, a god.

Fig bark
The bark of tropical fig trees. It was carefully removed, smoothed, and flattened to make Aztec folding books.

Flint
A hard stone formed in chalky soils. It can be carefully chipped, using stone hammers, to create axes, knives, and other sharp tools.

Flowery wars
Wars fought between the Aztecs and other peoples in Mexico. By fighting, the Aztecs hoped to win captives to sacrifice to their gods.

Guardian god
A god who protects a people or a place.

Incense
A sweet-smelling substance often burned in holy places such as temples.

Novice
A beginner or trainee.

Obsidian
A black, glassy stone produced when volcanoes erupt.

Overlords
People who rule over or control other peoples.

Mesoamerica
The region where North and South America meet. Today, Mesoamerica includes the countries of Mexico, Guatemala, Honduras, El Salvador, and Belize.

Picture-writing
A way of writing using pictures instead of letters.

Potion
A drink of medicine, poison, or supposedly magic liquid.

Ritual
A ceremony that is repeated at special times, such as during religious festivals.

Sacrifice
A person or animal that is killed as an offering, usually to the gods.

Scribe
Person trained in the skills of reading and writing Aztec picture-symbols.

Skull rack
A wood or stone rack, designed to contain hundreds of human skulls, that stood outside Aztec temples.

Tribute
Taxes paid in goods by conquered people to their conquerors.

Venus
One of the planets of the solar system. Like the Earth, it orbits the sun.

Xipe Totec
The Aztec god of fertility. He protected shoots of corn plants.

Index

Top Gods of the Aztec World

The list of Aztec gods is extremely long, and we may never fully understand this complex religion. Most gods had several different names, and their roles changed with the seasons. The most ancient gods were **Two Lord** and **Two Lady**, whose four sons in turn created all the other gods, the world, and the human race.

One of the four sons was **Tezcatlipoca**, which means Smoking Mirror. Other major deities included **Xipe Totec** (the Flayed God), **Huitzilopochtli** (Blue Hummingbird), **Quetzalcoatl** (Plumed Serpent), and the **Lords of the Night Sky**. Xipe Totec was usually shown wearing the skin of a sacrificed victim.

Each god was associated with, among other things, a direction, a color, a season, a day, a month, certain natural forces or events, and particular types of human behavior. **Tlaloc**, the god of rain, could bring drought and famine. **Ixtlilton** was the god of peaceful sleep. **Tlazolteotl** was the goddess of purification. **Mictlantecuhtli** was the fearsome god of death.

Many lesser gods were worshipped in different parts of the empire, including dozens of maize (corn) gods and several gods of *pulque* (an alcoholic drink made from the sap of the maguey, a species of agave plant).

Who Was Hernando Cortés?

In 1519, not long after the events described in the main part of this book, Spanish adventurer Hernando Cortés set out to conquer the Aztec empire. He used deception and cruel punishments, which included burning captives alive.

When Cortés landed in Mexico, he destroyed the ships he had arrived in, so that his men could not be tempted to retreat.

At first the Aztecs welcomed Cortés. But he captured Aztec emperor Montezuma, and brutally executed Aztec generals. The Aztecs fought back bravely, but their traditional weapons were powerless against European guns. By 1521, Cortés had conquered them. Other *conquistadores* (conquerors) followed. By 1600, most of South America was ruled by Spain.

Did You Know?

• This magnificent carved stone shows a
powerful Aztec prophecy that said the
world would end when the god
Quetzalcoatl arrived from across the
sea. For a while, Aztecs suspected that
Cortés might be this god. Because
horses were unknown in Mexico, the
Aztecs feared that Cortés's soldiers on horseback
might be magical monsters.
• The diseases spread by the conquerors, such as measles and
smallpox, were even more deadly than their weapons. By
around 1600, about five out of every six Aztecs had died.

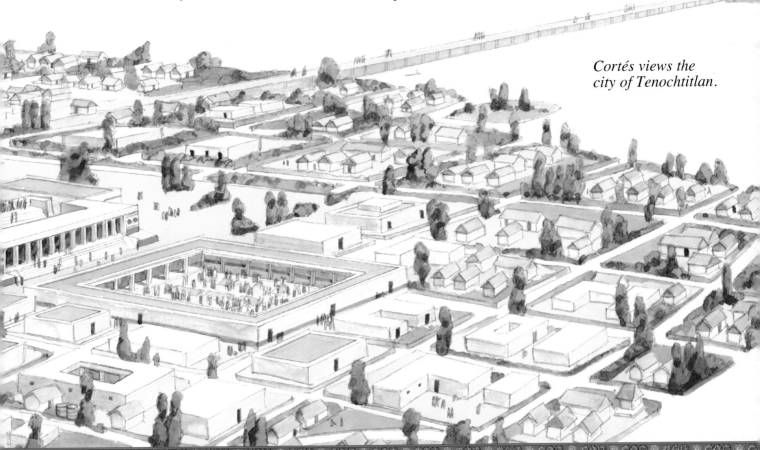

*Cortés views the
city of Tenochtitlan.*